The Roman Army: The History and Legacy of the Military that Revolutionized Ancient Warfare and Made Rome a Global Empire

By Charles River Editors

Rama's picture of a relief depicting a Roman legion

About Charles River Editors

Charles River Editors is a boutique digital publishing company, specializing in bringing history back to life with educational and engaging books on a wide range of topics. Keep up to date with our new and free offerings with [this 5 second sign up on our weekly mailing list](), and visit [Our Kindle Author Page]() to see other recently published Kindle titles.

We make these books for you and always want to know our readers' opinions, so we encourage you to leave reviews and look forward to publishing new and exciting titles each week.

Introduction

Christian Peter Marinescu-Ivan's picture of a recreation of a Roman soldier

The Roman Army

The Roman army is one of the most famous fighting forces in history. Through its power and prowess, a once obscure Italian city forged an empire that encircled the Mediterranean and covered half of Europe. The physical remains of its presence can be traced from the mountainous borders of Scotland to the arid deserts of Egypt, but its legacy is far greater and more enduring, as Rome's influence continues to shape the political, legal, and cultural landscape of Europe to this very day.

While the Roman army is rightly famed as an institution, the image of the individual legionary is also an iconic one. The uniformed, disciplined soldier of the late Republic and early Empire is one of the first things many people imagine when they think of Rome. They are the ultimate image of the ancient soldier, their arms and armor instantly recognizable. Their abilities, not only as warriors but also as engineers and administrators, have made them role models for other soldiers through the centuries. In the same vein, their commanders are still celebrated and studied, and generals the world over have tried to emulate the likes of Julius Caesar.

Of course, recruiting and equipping the Roman army were hardly easy tasks. Gathering new recruits wasn't difficult since service in the military was a requirement for social advancement, but new soldiers had to be trained to fight as heavy infantry and work together. For these men to be trained properly, however, they needed to have equipment, including swords, shields, javelins, helmets, and assorted armor. In addition to this, the new recruits had to be clothed, fed and paid, while commanders had to be found.

Moreover, one of the key ingredients to Rome's success was the military's complete willingness to incorporate discovered technologies. If a different weapon, type of armor, or basic equipment or artillery worked better than what they were using, the Romans were not afraid to adopt that piece of military hardware for their own uses. Thus, the Romans were almost always using the finest military equipment in the world, all of which had long since proven effective on the field of battle.

The Roman Army: The History and Legacy of the Military that Revolutionized Ancient Warfare and Made Rome a Global Empire examines the history of one of the most famous fighting forces in the world. Along with pictures depicting important people, places, and events, you will learn about the Roman army like never before.

The Roman Army: The History and Legacy of the Military that Revolutionized Ancient Warfare and Made Rome a Global Empire

About Charles River Editors

Introduction

   Predecessors

   A Citizen Army

   Transforming the Army

   Equipping the Army

   Officers

   Life in the Army

   Auxiliaries

   On the March

   Battle

   Civilian Roles

   Politics

   Online Resources

   Further Reading

Free Books by Charles River Editors

Discounted Books by Charles River Editors

Predecessors

Although the armies of the ancient Greek, or "Hellenic", city-states (*poleis*, singular *polis*) included both cavalry (*hippeis*) and light infantry (*psiloi, peltastes, gymnetes*), their mainstay was undoubtedly the heavy infantry known today as hoplites. Most historians believe that the hoplite became the dominant infantry soldier in nearly all the Greek city-states around the 8th century BCE. They fought in the tight phalanx formation, and beyond the confines of their small poleis, Greek hoplites were also prized as mercenaries throughout the ancient world.

Hoplites were responsible for acquiring their own equipment, so not every hoplite might have been equally armed, but considering the style of warfare, they needed as much uniformity as possible. Like most infantry outside of Greece, the hoplites also carried spears, but while the Persian weapons were short and light for example, the Greek spears were thick shafts anywhere between seven and nine feet long. These spears were topped by a 9-inch spearhead, with a "lizard-sticker" buttspike at the bottom which could be used as a secondary spearhead if the main weapon was snapped off, or to plant the spear upright when at rest. Each hoplite also carried a shortsword, designed specifically for thrusting in the close confines of a melee (the Spartan weapon, the *xiphos,* was so short as to be virtually a dagger, its blade barely over a foot long).

The hoplite's main offensive weapon was the spear *(dory)*. It was around 2-2.5 meters (roughly 6.5-8.5 feet) in length, and about five centimeters (2 inches) wide, although in later time periods it became longer. The *dory* was usually made of ash or cornel wood, with an iron or bronze spearhead counterbalanced by a butt-spike that allowed it to be planted in the ground as well as continue to be used in combat even after breaking. The hoplite often carried a second spear, as depicted in both art and literature, which could be used either for throwing or as a spare. As a secondary weapon, the hoplite also carried a sword called a *xiphos*, and possibly also a dagger or knife (*encheireidion*) (Lee: 483; Hanson 2000: 83-88; Anderson 1995).

The hoplite's main defensive weapon was the *aspis* or *hoplon.* This was a large, heavy wooden shield, sometimes covered in bronze, or simply reinforced with a bronze rim. From archaeological evidence and reconstructions, we know it was at least three feet in diameter and half an inch thick, weighing about 16 pounds. It was usually handled with the left hand. An innovative part of the hoplite's shield was the double "Argive" grip (named after the city-state of Argos) which included both a handle (*antilabe*) and a supporting leather fastening (*porpax*), allowing for far easier handling than other shields of the time (Lee: 481-483; Viggiano, Van Wees 2013: 57-60; Hanson: 65-71; Anderson).

The hoplite shield was very important in the Greek conception of warfare: the alternative name for the shield, *hoplon*, also refers to the entirety of the hoplite panoply (panoply= "*pan hoplon*", lit. "all weapons"), and provided the term *hoplite* itself. The hoplite's shield was often decorated with various symbols, such as the apotropaic "gorgoneion", the head of the legendary monster Medusa, who turned men to stone with her gaze and was killed by Perseus before being placed on the shield of the goddess Athena (Potts 1982: 26-28). Sometimes, the symbols were personal, while other times, they were common to whole cities, such as the letters Mu for Messene, Sigma for Sicyon, the Club of Hercules for Thebes, the owl of Athena for Athens in later times, or, most famously, the Lambda on the Spartan shield, which stood for Lacedaemon or Laconia, alternative names for the city (Vaughn 1993: 54; Ray 2011: 10).

It has been traditionally stated that, because of the shape of the hoplite shield, each man would not be fully covered by his own shield, but could provide protection to the man to his left, and would in turn require protection from the man on his right: this would mean that the *aspis* could only be used to its full potential in a tight formation (Viggiano, Van Wees: 57-58; Hanson: 27-28). Whether or not this is true, it speaks to the strong link between the *aspis* and the war-culture of the ancient Greek hoplite, centered on fighting in solidarity with a group rather than individual heroics. Furthermore, the dead were traditionally carried from the battlefield on their shields, while abandoning one's shield, as seen in Archilochus, was tantamount to fleeing battle: this gave rise to the saying of the Spartan women to their sons when they went to battle "return with your shield or on it" (Plutarch, *Moralia,* 241F).

Almost as iconic as the *aspis* is the "Corinthian" helmet (named after the city-state of Corinth), which covered almost the entire face, thus offering a lot of protection but potentially limiting the hearing and range of vision of its wearer. In depictions, the Corinthian helmet usually features an imposing plumed crest (Hanson: 71-75; Viggiano, Van Wees 60-61). Another part of hoplite's armor was the heavy bronze corselet protecting the torso, and greaves, as well as arm- and thigh-guards (Viggiano, Van Wees: 61-63; Hanson: 76-83).

Given that it was particularly costly for the average ancient Greek citizen, hoplite armor and weaponry was often passed down in a family. Furthermore, although artistic depictions tend to show hoplites in full armor, it is not certain that every ancient Greek hoplite could afford the full kit: arm and thigh guards, for example, were relatively rare, and the widespread usage of the bronze corselet cannot be proven. And even the iconic Corinthian helmet may more often than not, especially in later times when hoplite armor grew progressively lighter, have given way to a less showy but also far less expensive leather cap called the *pilos* (Viggiano, Van Wees: 61-63; Hanson: 70).

It has traditionally been thought that the limitations of hoplite equipment severely impeded the way in which hoplites fought, essentially making hoplites slow, static warriors who were only fully efficient in a tight formation, the famous *phalanx*. However, while it is undeniable that the weaponry of the hoplite affected the way in which he fought, more recent theories have argued that these limitations are exaggerated, and that hoplite warfare was in fact far more flexible and fast paced than most people give it credit for.

The main battle formation in which the ancient hoplites fought was the phalanx, a densely packed formation about eight men deep, although in later years it got much deeper. The front rank of a phalanx formed a wall of shields, while the spears were held out forward, or, in the ranks behind, above the men in front of them in order to provide protection from enemy missiles. As mentioned earlier, each hoplite was covered not only by his own shield, but also by that of the man next to him, to such an extent that hoplite phalanxes tended to shift to the right as men instinctively sought cover (Lee: 483; Hanson: 85). This allegedly led to the traditional practice of placing the best soldiers on the right to hold the phalanx in place.

An illustration depicting the phalanx formation

Herodotus records the running charge of the Greeks against the Persians at the battle of Marathon as the first of its kind (Herodotus, *Histories*, VI, 112), implying furthermore that the advance of the hoplite phalanx was generally slow. One can thus imagine the terrifying scene of a marching hoplite phalanx as the slow and inexorable advance of a surface of spears and shields, creating a "killing zone" directly in front of it within range of the spears. Neither the missile weapons of the time, nor the relatively light cavalry that existed in Greece, were particularly efficient against a phalanx in proper formation, thus largely relegating these troops to supporting roles. The phalanx formation was, however, vulnerable to attacks from the flank and difficult to maneuver or even maintain on non-level terrain.

Since hoplite phalanxes were the main type of military unit in most Greek poleis, war was generally decided in confrontations between phalanxes. These were a highly ordered affair, with the armies aligning themselves opposite to each other on a level plain. After offering a sacrifice to the gods and singing the *paean*, a traditional victory hymn to the god Apollo, the opposing phalanxes would march against each other. A highly significant part of the confrontation was the *othismos* (literally "pushing"), in which the hoplites of the front rows would push against each other, supported by the men behind them, each trying to break the other side's shield wall. Once one of the phalanxes broke ranks, its hoplites, much weaker outside of formation, could be mowed down easily by their opponents who were still holding their shield wall. The breaking of a phalanx generally meant the end of the battle. After the battle, the winner would set up a trophy (*tropaion*) with the weaponry of their defeated enemies. The losing side would request the right to bury their dead. This was generally granted, not only because it was sacrilegious to refuse, but also because the request itself was an admission of defeat, and thus an end to hostilities (Lee: 484; Hanson: 27-30).

Traditionally, inter-polis hoplite warfare has been seen by scholars as almost a ritual shoving match between opposing phalanxes, with strict rules and limited casualties as the fight was generally accepted to be over once the ranks broke. However, more recently, scholars have begun to question the accuracy of such representations. Raising doubts about the practicality of *othismos* as a war tactic, and taking the term when used in ancient texts to more generally to refer to the ebb and flow of battle, scholars like Van Wees and Viggiano redefine our view of hoplite warfare, especially in the earlier days. They take their cues both from ancient artistic representations—such as vase paintings representing hoplites in a variety of different battle poses, or the poems of the Spartan Tyrtaeus describing different sorts of fighting activities and fighters, including *psiloi*, taking part in battle together—as well as the ways in which war is fought in modern-day primitive societies with weapons similar to those of the hoplites (albeit far lighter and more crude). Their argument is that hoplite warfare was in fact far more flexible and fast-paced than we give it credit for, with men continually running to and from the battle, reinforcing the front line, pelting and avoiding projectiles, and even resting in between bouts of fighting (Vigianno, Van Wees: 63-72; Lee: 485-486; Anderson: 15-16; Krentz 2013).

The Spartans, due to the ferocity of their training and the intensity of their drill, were peerless at phalanx warfare. They were Greece's only full-time soldiers, with most other cities fielding citizen militias instead, so they avoided the traditional hoplite problem of edging to the right, into the "shadow" of their rankmate's shield. This edging meant that undisciplined formations often found themselves outflanked, and all armies, including the Spartans, fielded their elite unit (in the Spartans' case the *hippeis*) to the far right to keep the line steady. The left was traditionally reserved for the *skiritai*, the Spartan rangers, who considered it their post of honor.

During the Persian Wars (499-449 BCE), hoplites proved their superiority against vastly larger Persian forces in battles like Marathon (490 BCE) Thermopylae (480 BCE) and Plataea (479 BCE). And when Alexander the Great crossed the Hellespont into Asia in 334 BCE and conquered the Persian Empire, the largest state of its time, it was largely thanks to the hoplites of the new and improved Macedonian phalanx. When Alexander's kingdom was divided among his generals, the militaries of his successor states largely relied on the Macedonian phalanx, effectively making hoplite warfare the standard throughout most of the known world.

It was only with the advent of the more mobile Roman legion, and the defeat of phalanxes in battles like Cynoscephalae (197 BCE) and Pydna (168 BCE), that the hoplite phalanx was finally outclassed, although not without a long fight. The last of Alexander's successor kingdoms, Ptolemaic Egypt, only fell in 31 BCE.

A Citizen Army

The early days of the Roman army, like the rest of early Roman history, are shrouded in uncertainty. Surviving Roman records only come down from the 3rd century onward, and a great deal of mythology had already grown up by that point. Historians' understanding of the early army, therefore, comes from a mixture of archaeology, outside sources, and fragments of truth filtered from Rome's muddied mix of legend and oral history. Did Romulus, the founder of Rome, really exist? Did he have a bodyguard of 300 men, the precursor to the later legions? It's unlikely anyone will ever know for sure.

Rome's slow rise to power began around the 8th century BCE. At that point, Italy was a mass of small individual states. Aristocrats would lead bands to raid the neighboring settlements rather than great wars of conquest. Over time, this changed, as Rome began to conquer its neighbors or to dominate them so heavily that they were forced to become subservient allies.

During the first days of the Roman Republic, the military consisted of a militia. The men defending Rome and conquering her neighbors were not professional soldiers but Roman citizens called up to defend their home. Every citizen had a duty to fight and to equip himself for war, so the nature of that equipment depended upon his social standing, as wealthier men could afford better equipment.

The Roman soldiers of this period wore relatively simple bronze body armor. Their helmets mostly just protected the top of the head, not the sides or neck, and they were sometimes decorated with a tall, arrow-shaped plate rising out of the top. These early Romans fought with spears and shields.

Around the time that the armies of Rome first marched forth, hoplite tactics were being utilized across Greece, which brought about both social and tactical changes in the way armies worked. In contrast with how the Romans were fighting, the way the hoplites used their weapons was radically different. Since the hoplites fought in densely packed formations, each man's right side was protected by his neighbor's shield, allowing them to close on the enemy and use a bristling mass of spear points to overwhelm opponents and bring a quick, decisive win.

Hoplite tactics reached Italy via Greek colonies in the south of the peninsula. From there, this way of fighting was adopted by the Etruscans, and then by their neighbors and rivals, the Romans. Though hoplite formations looked very different from the Romans as people picture them today, it planted the seeds for the distinctive Roman way of war. Tightly packed troops created a tough shield wall that was hard for opponents to penetrate. Discipline was critical. Success was not attained through individual acts of courage but through working together as a formation.

This success was made possible by the growing wealth of Rome, since hoplite equipment wasn't cheap. Those who could afford it were mostly landowning farmers, men who wanted to uphold the security and stability of the state. These farmers gained political influence through their military role. The fact that Rome could put together an army like this meant that it had more land and more people than before.

Not everyone who fought in the hoplite army was a hoplite. The Servian system, named after a king in the 6th century BCE, laid down the equipment each soldier was meant to provide depending on their wealth. This ranged from the wealthy hoplites down to poor men carrying slings and stones. This system reflected the increasing standardization of the army, with units of set sizes and equipment. Military function, political influence, and personal wealth were closely tied.

The more systematic approach eventually led to the creation of a standard set of military formations, first recorded by Polybius in the 2nd century BCE, but which probably existed for over a hundred years before. In this Polybian system, a complete army was made up of six formations. Two units of cavalry sat on the flanks. Next to them were two alae, units made up of allied troops (precursors to the later auxiliaries). In the center were two legions made up of Rome's citizen soldiers.

Each legion consisted of 30 maniples divided into three lines.

In the front line were 10 maniples of hastati, the youngest legionaries. A hastati maniple contained 120 men, divided into two centuries of 60 men each. Each century was led by a centurion and standard bearer at the front, with a junior officer called an optio at the back to keep the ranks in order.

Behind the hastati came 10 maniples of principes, men in their 20s and 30s. These were the backbone of the legion, organized in the same way as the hastati.

The last line consisted of the triarii. These were the most experienced soldiers. Their maniples contained only 60 men, thereby relying on skill rather than numbers.

These formations were all equipped in the same way. Each legionary had an oval shield, a sword called a gladius, and two javelins to throw before going into close combat. The rear formations had long spears, a holdover from the days of hoplite fighting. All wore helmets and body armor.

At that time, the Romans were using tactics that would lead them to dominate the region within. They fought in tightly packed, disciplined formations as the hoplites did, but instead of presenting a mass of spear points, they threw their spears at close range, disrupting enemy formations before attacking with short swords.

This was the army with which Rome defeated Carthage, its leading competitor in the Mediterranean, during the Punic Wars in the 3rd and 2nd centuries BCE. As Roman territory increased, a standardized militia allowed the Romans to quickly mobilize large armies and win wars without suffering terrible losses.

However, expansion exposed problems within the militia system. Farms lay neglected as their owners went to war, sometimes for years at a time, which disrupted the local economy and left legionaries in financial trouble upon their return. Permanent armies were needed to garrison distant and restive parts of the empire, further straining the militia system. Those who fought began to resent the system that recruited them, even as it struggled to hold the empire together.

Something had to change.

Transforming the Army

The pressure of war with Carthage and governing a growing empire led to another wave of military reform. These changes took place in the late 2nd century and are often attributed to one man, Gaius Marius.

A bust of Marius

In 107 BCE, Marius was the commander of a war in Africa. He knew that he would need fresh troops, but he was not allowed to raise new legions, only volunteers. Thus, he reached out to the lowliest of Rome's citizens, men who had previously been too poor to equip themselves and fight, and called upon them to join him. Many seized the opportunity and signed up, providing Marius with an army that was as effective as the ones that existed before.

It is not clear whether Marius was a revolutionary trying something new or whether he formalized a change that had already been brewing, but it is clear that his actions permanently transformed the relationship between the army and Roman society. Instead of a volunteer militia made up of men wealthy enough to equip and support themselves, the legions were now made up of professional soldiers, paid and equipped by the state. These legionaries did not head home at the end of each campaign but stayed in service for 25 years. This meant that they built up training and experience, becoming an increasingly effective fighting force. Though officers were still drawn from the aristocracy, there was now some continuity in command, especially at the lower level, where unit leaders were drawn from among the rank-and-file.

Legionaries still had to be Roman citizens, but the pool of citizens became far larger. Following the Social War of 91-88 BCE, most of the Italians under Roman rule were made citizens of Rome, mostly in order to prevent another revolt. With that, legionaries could be recruited from almost anywhere in the peninsula.

Alongside the transformation of who fought, Marius oversaw a change in the way the troops were organized. An army was now made up of a variable number of legions supported by auxiliary forces, and the Italian allies who had previously made up the alae formations were brought into the legions themselves.

Each legion was made up of 10 cohorts. They still fought in three lines, but every cohort had the same number of men and the same equipment. This provided more flexibility than the previous system, in which each formation had to be part of a specific line.

The fundamental unit of the legion was a century, a unit of 80 men organized into four ranks. They were led by a centurion and a standard bearer at the front, with an optio, a lower ranking officer than the centurion, at the back to keep the men in line. Each cohort had six centuries. These cohorts were large enough to fight independently if needed, but still small enough to provide flexibility in the way units were fielded.

A single eagle standard replaced the five different standards each legion had previously followed.

Naturally, professional soldiers had to be provided with standardized equipment, and Marius ensured that this was done. Each legionary had the same armor and weapons as the men next to him. He carried all the kit he would need to camp and to feed himself, as well as tools for construction. Weighed down by a great amount of equipment while marching back and forth across the empire, these men became known as Marius's mules.

Mocking as that nickname might sound, the men of the post-Marian legions took great pride in their work. In addition to their impressive martial skills, they were taught construction and engineering, enabling them to build bridges, roads, and military camps. They worked together for years on end in units that were now made permanent, which ensured unit pride became deeper and more ingrained than under the militia system. There had always been a sense of pride attached to serving in the Roman legions. Initially, it was the pride of volunteers bravely leaping to defend their homeland, and now it was the pride of poor men given profession and purpose through military service. Legionaries depended upon the army for their livelihood, rather than having their livelihood threatened by the disruption of military service. This transformed their relationship with war and with the men who led them. Men inevitably became attached not only to their fellow soldiers but also their commanders, which would have profound consequences in the 1st century BCE.

Patronage was a fundamental part of Roman society, with the wealthy elite earning the support of the poor by helping them out when they were in need or by putting forward political agendas that would appeal to the masses. A wealthy senator might have a huge number of clients loyal to him and dependent upon him for their livelihood and influence.

The professional army gave patronage a new edge. The Roman Senate was inherently conservative, and despite the transformation of the army into a professional body, it kept treating it as if it were a volunteer militia. No provision was made for men leaving the army, and if it happened, they lost their homes, income, and sense of purpose. It was here that commanders stepped into the breach. Many of them provided their men with plots of land when they left the army so that they could become farmers. Their concern for the needs of their men made them popular with soldiers and veterans who had served under them, creating a fresh web of patronage.

Of course, this could prove to be a dangerous form of patronage for the existing order, since a leading politician might gain the support of an entire army of trained, disciplined soldiers, as well as mobs of grateful ex-soldiers back home. Generals held huge influence, making the army an important player in the troubled internal politics of Rome.

Equipping the Army

Weapons

The legionaries, the core troops of the post-Marian Roman army, were equipped with a standard set of weapons, armor, and uniform. Although the exact designs evolved, the general way they were equipped remained remarkably stable for centuries.

The most important weapon carried by any legionary was the gladius, a type of short sword. It had a blade between 40 and 55 centimeters long (16 to 22 inches) and a single-handed handle. This short design made it easy to be carried on the right-hand side and easily drawn there, avoiding the need to draw it across the body and so risk getting entangled with a shield. The shortness also made the blade suitable for close quarters fighting, where it could be used to stab and thrust in a small space.

The type of gladii used during the early Roman era is now referred to as Mainz-pattern gladii. These well-balanced swords had a long point that made them effective both for slashing and for stabbing. The Pompeii-pattern gladius took its place during the 1st century CE. Even better balanced than its predecessor, the Pompeii gladius was also more standardized in length, reflecting the increasing professionalism and organization of the Roman army.

A Pompeii-pattern gladius

Legionaries also carried a throwing spear called a pilum. Their designs varied more than those of the swords. Some included a weight behind the head that gave the pilum extra momentum and so more power to punch through armor. With an effective range of around 15m (50ft), pilums were held back until the last moment, then thrown at enemy troops just before the two sides clashed.

Cristian Chirita's picture of a relief of legionaries carrying pilums

Historians used to believe that legionaries usually carried two javelins, but there is little evidence for this. Most troops probably only carried a single pilum.

Armor

Like the image of a soldier with two throwing spears, the iconic image of Roman armor does not reflect what most legionaries wore. Throughout Roman history, the most widely used armor was chainmail. Usually made from iron, it was a shirt of hundreds of interlocking rings between one and seven millimeters thick. It provided good protection, especially against slashing blows, but swift sword or spear thrusts could burst the links and so pierce the armor, as could arrows fired at short range.

Lorica segmentata, the style of armor usually associated with Roman armies, was used by some of the legions between the 1st and 3rd centuries CE. A set of overlapping metal plates, provided greater protection while still having some flexibility. Another alternative for Roman soldiers was scale male, metal scales sewn onto cloth in overlapping layers.

All legionaries wore helmets, but their design varied from place to place and over time. Features common at the height of the empire included broad cheek guards to protect the sides of the face and another plate at the back protecting the neck. The top of the helmet and the forehead often had bars or ridges to provide more solid protection, as this was where legionaries were most likely to be hit while protected by their large shields.

During the days of the Republic, it was common to wear decorative helmet crests into battle. Under the principate and the empire, helmets kept crest fittings so that they could be made more impressive for parades, but the crests were seldom worn in battle.

For centuries, Roman legionaries carried the same type of shield. Tall and semi-cylindrical with straight sides, it provided protection for most of the body. When a group of legionaries stood firmly together, these shields created a virtual wall blocking their enemies. The shields were made from wooden strips glued on top of each other in layers, often reinforced with metal bindings. The handle was a horizontal grip behind a central metal boss.

Most Roman men, civilian or soldier, wore a tunic. During the early days of the army, legionaries wore their own mismatched tunics under their armor. As standard military equipment was developed, matching tunics were brought in, providing the legions with a uniform appearance.

Most tunics were made by stitching together two squares of wool or linen up the sides and across the top, leaving holes for the head and arms. The difference between military and civilian tunics was that the ones worn by soldiers were longer, though this did not usually show, as they were hitched up above the knees for ease of movement.

Belts were an important symbol. They were used to hitch up the long tunics, and it was easy to distinguish soldiers from other people even when not in uniform. Standing unbelted could be used as a punishment, signaling a soldier's disgrace.

More than this, a belt was important for carrying the rest of a soldier's equipment. It spread the weight of chainmail away from the shoulders, making it easier to wear for extended periods. Swords, knives, and pouches all hung from the belt.

Cloaks were vitally important for staying warm and dry while on the march or standing as a sentry in all kinds of weather. Legionaries wore two styles of cloak - a rectangle of wool held by a brooch at the right shoulder, called a sagum, and an oval with a hole for the head and toggles fastening the front, called a paenula. The paenula sometimes included a hood.

Good footwear was essential for an army on the march. The caliga was the standard Roman military shoe, a cross between a boot and a sandal. It had a sole fitted with metal studs to improve the grip and wear, an insole, an upper, and straps that could be tightened for a close fit. The sandal-like open upper gave way to more enclosed designs in the 2nd century CE. For added warmth, legionaries wore socks under their boots.

Legionaries spent a lot of time working on construction projects, including military camps, siege works, and civilian infrastructure. For this, they carried a variety of construction tools.

Josephus, a historian of the 1st century CE, provided a long list of tools that every legionary supposedly carried. This included an axe, basket, bill-hook, chain, pick, saw, and strap. This was clearly more than any single soldier could practically carry, so it was probably the set of equipment for a group of legionaries, with each of them carrying a tool or two. Specialist tools were also important but rarer; for example, only a few men in any army would need a groma, an instrument used for surveying.

Officers

A clear hierarchy of officers in the Roman army made them orderly. Even under the emperors, when the senate no longer ran the empire, those filling senior positions were normally men from the senatorial class, Rome's clearly defined elite.

The most senior position was that of legatus Augusti proparetore. This was the military commander who was also the governor of a province, a role that combined the military and political aspects of most senators' careers. Such posts were few and far between, the peak of a successful career, and usually lasted around three years.

The next most senior post was that of legatus legionis, the commander of a legion, a force of around 5,000 men. Such positions usually went to senators in their thirties who had focused on the military side of their careers.

The legatus legionis's deputy was the tribunus laticlavius. This was the most junior role regularly occupied by someone from a senatorial family, the first step in a young nobleman's military career. This role was usually served by youth in their late teens or early twenties and served for only a year, gaining some military experience before being given a civilian position.

Next in the hierarchy of a legion came the camp prefect, the praefectus castrorum. This more hands on role was given to a former chief centurion, a veteran soldier with a lifetime of experience under his belt, to ensure the smooth running of the camp. It was the only way that a man of humble background could reach such a position of responsibility in Roman society.

The equestrians, the second tier of Rome's social elite, had their own military career path separate from that of the senators.

The first step was to become praefecti or prefect of an auxiliary infantry cohort. This was a far less prestigious post than commanding legionaries but had its advantages. An auxiliary cohort might be the only Roman force for miles around, giving the praefecti a chance to show initiative and prove himself.

The next step for a successful praefecti was to become a tribunus angusticlavii, a position similar to a modern staff officer. There were five positions like this in each legion, giving equestrian officers a chance to work with the military elite and impress their senatorial superiors. They might even get to command legionaries if a group was sent off as a vexillation, a detachment separated from the legion for a specific task.

After serving in a legion, an equestrian officer could then move on to the most senior post available to him - praefecti of an auxiliary cavalry unit. Cavalry were more prestigious than other auxiliaries and so this was a good position for an ambitious career officer to hold.

The leadership of the army was dominated by the senatorial and equestrian social classes, the men of Rome's powerful elite. But there was a significant exception - the centurions. These were usually men of humbler background who had proved themselves as legionaries and been trusted with a position of command.

A centurion was the commander of a century, a unit of 80 legionaries, or an equivalent group of auxiliaries. The century was the fundamental unit of the Roman army, large enough to have an impact in battle but small enough to be deployed swiftly and flexibly. All the other formations of the army were made up of centuries. A centurion would normally command his unit as part of a larger cohort, made up of six centuries. But a century would sometimes be called upon to act independently, with its centurion in command. Centurions, therefore, had to be able to act on their own initiative just as readily as they followed the commands of others.

Luc Viator's picture of a reenactor dressed as a centurion

Not all centurions were equal, and there were a number of different positions within this class of officer. Within each legion, the centurions of the first cohort held the highest rank, the title of primi ordines. Some centurions came from the equestrian class, taking this post because they could not get a more prestigious one. Some were veterans of the elite praetorian guard, who could become centurions of other units after 16 years in the guard. But the route to power most associated with centurions was a rise through the ranks. Through proven experience or bold acts of courage, ordinary legionaries could be promoted to command a century.

Centurions led from the front. Experienced and highly trained, they set an example of courage and skill, as well as being a hard-hitting fighting elite. It was one of the reasons why they had a relatively high mortality rate. Many had gained their positions by courageously putting their lives on the line. To retain their posts, they kept trying to prove themselves, leading charges and entering the thick of the fighting. The rank of centurion was not suited to an armchair commander.

Since so many centurions were long-serving veterans, they had knowledge and experience of what was likely to happen, and officers turned to them for insight. Julius Caesar's councils of war included centurions such as Publius Sextius Baculus, one of the few men other than himself who Caesar took the time to praise.

At the peak of the empire, there were around 1,800 legionary centurions and at least as many working with the auxiliaries. Those who survived this dangerous role gained wealth and prestige inaccessible to ordinary citizens of the empire. They returned home as people of significance and as inspiration to young men in their communities. Their prestige helped ensure that the young men followed their path and entered the legions.

Life in the Army

By joining the Roman army, a man would be committed to a very different life from the ordinary one. He would sometimes be in constant service for years, his wake-up time regulated by the rules of military life.

Men's lives depended upon each other's actions, and the fate of the empire was at stake. The punishment for indiscipline could therefore be severe. Falling asleep on guard duty could see a man put to death, and most famously, if a unit dishonored itself through a particularly heinous battlefield failure, it would be subjected to decimation. For a decimation, 1 out of every 10 of the men were picked out at random, and the rest of the unit, men with whom they had built up friendships over years of service, were forced to beat them to death.

Like many empires, the Romans sent their soldiers far from their native lands. This gave the state and its officers more control over them. An African legion based in Africa would have local connections and might get caught up in local politics or even a revolt, whereas an African legion station on Hadrian's Wall, far away at the northern frontier, would have no local connections, making it entirely dependent upon the army for support and purpose.

As with any army, the everyday lives of Roman legionaries were far from glamorous. Routine duties made up 90% of a soldier's life, interspersed by the occasional moments of excitement and danger that came with war. Those at permanent military bases often lived in long barracks blocks. The eight men of a squad would share a room, sleeping in bunk beds. They would also have a room for their equipment, including clothes, tools, and weapons.

The day started with a breakfast of porridge or bread. Most of the food eaten by Roman armies was grain, livened up with the occasional vegetable or piece of meat. They carried sacks of grain or flour when they went on the march to ensure that they had enough food to keep them going.

After breakfast, the legionaries would muster on the parade ground. This was a chance for roll call, to check for desertion or sickness. Without modern medicine, everyone had to worry about illnesses, especially when living in a climate far hotter or colder than the land he called home. The troops were counted, inspected, and then assigned tasks for the day.

Duty on a military base varied. There were obvious and highly visible tasks, like guard and sentry duty, standing for hours at a time in full uniform and armor while watching out for any signs of trouble. There was "boots," time dedicated to maintaining equipment. This meant fixing, polishing, and caring for the possessions of officers, as well as those belonging to the soldiers themselves, from their weapons and armor to their tunics and sandals. And then there were the mundane tasks needed to maintain any community - repairing buildings, cooking food, and cleaning latrines.

A Roman military base was relatively hygienic. The Romans understood the importance of sewers and bathing, even though they didn't know about the effect of germs and cleanliness on good health. Not every base had a sewage system, but there were often pipes carrying waste from the toilet block into pits, which would have to be regularly emptied. If the base was large enough then there would be a bathhouse, where the men could enjoy cleaning and relaxing, just as they did in Rome.

There were military doctors to help keep the men healthy. They were generally well-regarded and many held the rank of centurion. Greece, one of the ancient world's great centers for medical learning, provided many of the doctors who worked for the Roman army.

Training was a regular part of life in the legions, though how regular depended upon how diligent the commanding officer was. Soldiers practiced marching, javelin throwing, and fighting with blunt weapons. They learnt to use the artillery that supported them on the battlefield and during sieges. They fought in mock battles and practiced laying out and building marching camps. Auxiliaries had a chance to practice their specialist skills such as archery and mounted combat.

Army bases were responsible for controlling an area, and this was reflected in the other activities the soldiers undertook. There were patrols of the surrounding country, ensuring the borders were safe, reminding people all over the empire of the authority of Rome. Legionaries maintained order in the areas where they were based and their officers were called upon to settle legal disputes. Their presence was not always welcomed, but it brought stability, security, and peace.

Religion and ceremony were important to life in the legions. Remains of shrines have been found at a number of military bases. There were many days of official celebration endorsed by the state, and these were recognized with parades, speeches, and ceremonies in military camps. Dates such as the celebration of Julius Caesar, associated with military glory and imperial success, were particularly important to military men. Sacrifices were made and feasts were held.

Nobody can know for sure what ordinary legionaries believed, but scholars have a good grasp of what gods were recognized within the empire and which were considered important in war. Mars, the god of war, was obviously significant, and over time, the cult of Mithras also became popular among soldiers. Mithras was worshipped not in public ceremonies but in private meetings of his followers, and a person had to be initiated into the cult to take part. This gave the cult a sense of mystery, which added to its popularity, at least until Christianity began to replace the old religions in the later days of the empire. By then, legionaries were among those spreading the new monotheistic faith across Europe.

In addition to shrines, many legionary forts had amphitheatres. These were used for blood sports and gladiatorial games such as those seen in Rome. Though less impressive than the games at the capital, these provided exciting entertainment and a break from the regular routine.

Auxiliaries

The legionaries are the most famous in the Roman armies, but another group of soldiers called the auxiliaries made up a large part of the forces of Rome. The auxiliaries weren't native Romans or citizens of the empire. They were recruited from the populations of conquered territories or from allies providing support to Rome. They worked for pay and for the opportunity to become Roman citizens, earning the privileges of imperial life through their work and sacrifice.

The auxiliaries were a diverse group when it came to their origins, equipment, and place in the army. Roman generals often made use of the specialist skills of particular regions. Cavalry were recruited from among the Celtic tribes, and from the Balearic Islands came sling-wielding missile troops. Archers were recruited from Crete during the Republican era, then later from the eastern Mediterranean and Syria, as these lands fell under the influence of an expanding empire.

Auxiliary units were generally smaller than those of the legions, which had two benefits. One was that they could be used more flexibly, with small groups being moved to different parts of the empire as they were needed. The other was control. The auxiliaries weren't bound to Rome as strongly as the legionaries were, so their loyalty could not be equally trusted. Smaller units would be easier to put down if they rebelled against their masters.

Of course, the auxiliaries did not have the same prestige as their legionary comrades. Records of the Roman army often leave out or minimize their part, whether in written accounts of battles or in visual depictions of the army in action. The proportion of auxiliaries on Trajan's Column, one of the greatest surviving depictions of the army, is not representative of their numbers within the armies of Rome. They are shown as mere background figures in the achievements of the legions.

A relief of the army from Trajan's Column

Though not as disciplined or well-equipped as legionaries, auxiliaries were not a disorganized rabble. They were distinct units with their own uniforms and ways of fighting, and their work earned them wealth and status. Moreover, when they returned home with the money they had made, they brought Roman culture to their people.

One of the most important groups of auxiliary troops was the archers. For much of Roman history, archery was not seen as a suitable form of combat for a Roman citizen. However, missile troops could be incredibly valuable in both battles and sieges, so they were recruited through the auxiliaries. Caesar used archers from Crete, but later they were drawn mostly from the Middle East, where there was a strong tradition of archery, influenced in part by Asian steppe nomads.

Roman archers used composite bows, which were made from layers of bone, horn, wood, and sinew, all glued and bound together. By using stiffer materials at the hand grip and the ends, bow makers added extra leverage through the string and reduced bucking when the bow was fired, making it more accurate. This led to weapons that were both strong and springy, with a lot of power despite their size.

Accompanying the bows were arrows made of reed or wood with a range of heads to suit different circumstances. Narrowly pointed bodkin arrows were used against opponents with heavy armor, such as those they faced in the east. The narrow point meant that the power of the shot was more focused, increasing the chances of piercing the armor. Against the tribesmen of central Europe and other unarmored foes, broad arrow heads were a better option, as their slicing action did more damage, cutting flesh and veins.

Archers carried swords in case they got involved in close quarters fighting, and they were armored in leather or chainmail. Wrist braces and finger guards protected them from injuries from their own bowstrings.

The range of missile weapons in the ancient world was quite limited, and this shaped the way archers were used. Their bows could fire 165-230 meters, but they were only effective at 50-150 meters. They were often placed behind the legionaries, firing over their heads with large volleys meant to disrupt and weaken enemy formations before the infantry attacked.

The exact way they were deployed varied with the commander. Caesar usually used them defensively, protecting the flanks or screening against cavalry. In his war against the Jews, Vespasian used them as an independent force, withstanding attacks and seizing high ground from which to fire on the enemy.

Horsemen were an important part of the army, used for scouting, skirmishing, guarding the flanks, and pursuing broken foes. The cavalry, therefore, had a more prestigious position than the rest of the auxiliaries, as reflected in the more senior rank given to equestrian officers when they commanded cavalry. Though still not as prestigious as the legionaries, they outshone the other auxiliaries.

Mounted recruits came from across the Roman world. During Caesar's Gallic Wars alone, he used cavalry from Gaul, Germany, and Spain.

Cavalry formations were called alae, like the old allied formations. They consisted of either 512 or 768 men, divided into 32-man units called turmae.

Like the legionary infantry, cavalrymen wore either chainmail or scale armor. Their helmets were a little different from those of the infantry, having more protection on the sides of the face as well as deeper and narrower neck guards. They carried flat shields, usually rectangular or oval.

Instead of the short gladius, cavalry carried a long sword called a spatha. This gave them extra reach, which was needed for fighting from horseback. They also used spears, some of them javelins to throw at the enemy, and some short stabbing spears for close combat. In a few cases, they did not carry shields but instead had a two-handed spear called a contus. This was 12 feet long and used for high impact charges, but it was only ever carried by a few specialist troops.

Roman cavalry did not have stirrups as modern riders do. They relied on four-horned saddles made out of metal, wood, and leather to give them a stable platform from which to fight.

On the March

Roman armies spent a lot of time on the march, which is not surprising given that they had a vast empire to maintain and threats to fend off on every side. Even when civil war broke out, it was seldom restricted to the imperial heartland.

The boots of Roman soldiers had metal studs, which gave them more grip and durability, but there was so much marching that even these became worn away. During the 1st century CE, a group of sailors from the imperial fleet appealed to Emperor Vespasian for money to replace their studs, as they had become worn away through long marches between Rome and its ports. Exacerbating the issue was the fact that the legionaries also carried a lot of equipment. Each man had to carry his own armor, clothes, weapons, and a bag of flour. Each unit had a set of construction tools and camping equipment distributed among its members.

Often amounting to tens of thousands of men, a Roman army could easily run into delays if it didn't stay organized. The order of march and discipline within that order were therefore very important. Troops would leave camp in a set order each morning so that they were in formation from the start.

A record of the marching order of Emperor Vespasian in Galilee reveals the sort of considerations that shaped a marching column. Lightly equipped auxiliaries were sent ahead to scout out the route and reveal any ambushes the enemy had planned. These were followed by a contingent of heavy troops in case of trouble. Then came the men carrying the equipment needed to lay out and set up a new camp at the end of the day, and those with tools to straighten the road and clear obstructions for the main column.

After the troops preparing the way, the next part of the formation was made up of the commander, his staff, and his baggage. Then came the cavalry and the siege train. Behind them, the infantry followed in order of prestige - the officers, then the legions, and finally the auxiliaries. A rearguard of mixed cavalry and infantry looked out for any trouble behind them. Not every army exactly followed Vespasian's formation, but it demonstrates the care and organization put into the marching army.

Roman armies often found themselves on the march in hostile territory. When they stopped for the night, they did not simply pitch tents and set sentries. They built fortified camps to keep them safe.

Preparations for the camp started while the army was still moving. A tribune and several centurions, experienced soldiers with a good eye for the land, were sent ahead as a surveying group. They looked for a suitable place to camp, somewhere at least 700 meters square so that it could hold all the troops and supplies. This would ideally be on a raised ground without any cover to create a strong defensive position and see enemies approaching from far. An enemy would be detected as far as four kilometers away. A water source was vital, one that the enemy could not foul or divert.

Having found a site, the surveying team began marking out the layout on which the camp would be built. They used a white flag to show where the commander's tent would be set up and a red flag to show the direction of the water source. Walls, roads, and areas for tents were all mapped out.

When the legionaries reached the site, construction began. Every unit carried a selection of tools and a bundle of sharpened stick that could be turned into a fence. They dug a ditch around the camp three feet deep, then built an earth rampart behind it topped with a wooden barricade or fence. Every maniple was given a specific section of the defenses to build, unless there were enemies nearby, in which case some men kept guard while others did the digging and building.

Once the defenses were built, the army gathered together and swore the camp oath, promising to follow the rules set out for life in camp. Then the legionaries pitched their tents, with one group also setting up the commander's area. Each unit had a set place within the camp layout, so they knew where to pitch their tents. They could get on with the task quickly and without disagreements over who got the best spots.

Guards were set not only to watch for people approaching the camp but to keep watch inside, in case of saboteurs or indiscipline. They guarded the commander's tent, the horses, and the supplies. Units patrolled the area. A password, distributed by four officers around dusk, let them check whether anyone they met was meant to be in the camp.

While the guards patrolled, the rest of the men cooked, ate, cleaned their equipment, and slept.

A blast from a horn woke up the camp the next morning. Guards reported anything unusual that had happened in the night. A cavalry patrol scouted the area for enemy troops and what they were doing. Then the commander called his officers together to advise him before he decided on their next move.

If the army stayed still, the day was spent reinforcing the camp's defenses. If not, another horn blast signaled the troops to pack up. Anything they could not carry was loaded onto mules. The third blast indicated that they should march out. The units left in a specific order based on their location in the camp, ensuring that they could leave with the minimum of fuss and congestion.

Most of the time, the main purpose of marching camps was to maintain order and discipline, but their defenses were sometimes invaluable. In 57 BCE, the Nervii and their allies attacked an army led by Caesar as he made camp in Gaul. The legionaries abandoned their tools, grabbed their weapons, and defended the camp. As this made clear, an army on the march was always ready for battle.

Battle

The skill of Roman commanders wasn't just about what they did on the battlefield. Finding the right battlefield and forcing the enemy to face them there was just as important as what they did on the field.

Rome's large, disciplined formations were best suited to fighting on large areas of open ground, so commanders sought such places to fight, often using raised ground or other terrain features to anchor their flanks and prevent the enemy from getting around them. At the Battle of Pharsalus in 48 BCE, Caesar stationed his army on the left side of the Enipeus River, which prevented Pompey's army from getting around him and allowed Caesar to win despite having the smaller army.

The defeat of the British Queen Boudicca in 60 CE was achieved through similarly careful use of terrain. Caius Suetonius Paulinus, the Roman governor of the province, formed up his army between two areas of wooded high ground through which it would be difficult to move troops. The Britons attacked him head-on, were unable to bring their superior numbers to bear, and became crammed in together when the Romans counterattacked. The British army was crushed, ending the revolt.

Forcing the enemy to face the Romans on their terms was not always easy. Sometimes Caesar would form up on defensive ground that his opponents were unlikely to attack. This way, he could put off fighting until a more auspicious occasion. The failure of these enemies to attack boosted his men's morale by encouraging them to believe that the enemy feared them.

The Roman army was designed for fighting pitch battles, and it was here that the structure, training, and equipment of the legions were on best display. Following the skills they had acquired on the training ground, the cohorts formed up in disciplined lines. Each legion formed up with four cohorts in the front line, three in the second, and three in the third. Gaps between the cohorts created space for units to move in and out of the battle line. The second line was quite likely to move forward in the course of the battle, while the third was held in reserve in case of crisis.

Within the cohort, the men were lined up four ranks deep. Each century was led by its own centurion, these seasoned officers leading from the front. The standard bearers of the centuries also stood in front of them, giving a clear point behind which to assemble and for the men to follow as they advanced.

Cavalry, most of them auxiliaries, formed up on the flanks of the army. Their job was to prevent flanking maneuvers and if possible to outflank the enemy. They could be used to pursue a broken enemy army as it ran.

Archers and other missile-wielding auxiliaries were used in different ways depending on the circumstances. They were often behind the main line of the legions, firing over their heads to break up the enemy formations before a charge.

The legionaries advanced in tight formation. This made their units easy targets for missiles, but they held their shields in front of them for protection, establishing a solid defensive wall. This was one of the reasons why good marching discipline was so important, as it helped keep the shield wall intact.

The only people out of formation were the senior officers and the messengers they used to send orders around the battlefield. Orders were transmitted down the chain of command to the centurions, who were responsible for ordering their units.

Once they were close enough to the enemy, the legionaries would throw their pilums. The weight of these javelins gave them a good chance of penetrating armor and shields, taking men down and breaking up their formations. This attack was therefore saved until the last second so that they could make the most impact. As the javelins fell, the legionaries charged. With their short swords, they were equipped to fight as close up as possible, right in their enemy's faces. The short blade of a gladius let a legionary thrust and stab even in a small, confined space, even while keeping his shield up to protect him.

Discipline was still crucial; victory in a battle like this was about keeping the army together and in the field. The legionaries had to keep their nerve and keep their line intact until the enemy's courage faltered and they ran. If the initial attack didn't work, the legions might pull back and wait for another chance. Superior discipline and training let them maneuver formations even in the heat of battle.

Commanders usually led from behind the lines, but not so far behind that they couldn't quickly make contact with their troops. Some commanders fought alongside their men during times of crisis, and Caesar took up arms on several occasions. Such actions put the commander's life at risk, but they helped to bolster the morale of the troops and increase their affection for their generals.

Though the Romans were formidable on the open battlefield, they truly excelled was in siege warfare. Many fortresses and walled cities fell before the might of Rome, and by laying siege to the enemy, the legions could combine their martial and engineering skills to break even the most determined of opponents.

Before starting a siege, the general had to make sure he had all the materials and manpower needed. Before Fulvius besieged Ambracia in 189 BCE, he checked that the local area contained all the raw materials needed to build his siege works and that there was a river that could bring his army's supplies. When Emperor Julian assembled a military expedition on the Euphrates in 363 CE, he made sure to bring siege materials as well as combat supplies and food.

Having surveyed the terrain and chosen the best ground, the Romans built a defensible camp, just as they did while on the march. This protected them from sorties made by the defenders in an attempt to break the siege. At Sparta in 195 BCE and Jerusalem in 70 CE, these attacks came before the Romans had even finished constructing the camp, showing why these defenses were so necessary.

Many towns had buildings outside their walls, as growing populations spread beyond a settlement's original boundaries. In these cases, the Romans would demolish these outer buildings. This created open ground for them to move and fire through. Materials from the demolished buildings could also be used in building their fortified camps and siege machines.

The threat of sorties meant that, during the preparatory stage, the Romans had to be careful to screen construction work from attacks. Sometimes natural features such as rivers and hills protected them. Sometimes it was a force of soldiers waiting and ready to fight. At Munda in 45 BCE, corpses from a nearby battlefield were turned into a temporary defensive barrier while the proper siege lines were being built.

Having established themselves close to an enemy town, the Romans' next step was to cut that settlement off from the outside world. For the armies of the early Republic, the best way to do this was a blockade camp. The blockade camp was a more substantial and resilient version of the regular marching camp. It was protected by ditches and solid walls topped with barricades or spikes. It provided a safe base for the besieging army, somewhere they could rest and from where they could launch attacks against any troops coming out of the city. Situated close to transport routes, it also cut the town off from supplies.

It was common to have more than one fortified camp as part of a blockade, covering routes in and out in multiple directions. These camps could be completely separate or could be connected by lines of barricades that provided an extra obstacle for opponents and cover for troops moving between bases.

Over time, a more advanced technique evolved from the blockade camps. This was circumvallation, the construction of a ring of defenses all the way around the besieged settlement. This was a far more complex and arduous undertaking than a blockade camp, but one with greater benefits. Circumvallation didn't just let the Romans cut off supply caravans and reinforcements approaching the city, it prevented even individual messengers from sneaking in and out.

Circumvallation often involved building two lines of defenses - one facing the city and the other facing away, in case of an attack by a relief force. The besieging Roman army lived between these two lines of defenses in something like a ring-shaped fort. Artillery and archers used turrets and ramparts within the siege lines to fire at the town's defenders, adding to the pressure of the siege.

Reconnaissance was vital, as a lack of understanding could bring problems. Censorinus's siege of Carthage in 149 BCE was severely hampered by making camp next to a stagnant lagoon full of disease. Conversely, it was through a careful reconnaissance that Caesar learned that he could not build a siege line all around Avaricum in 52 BCE and would have to achieve victory through a blockade camp.

The most famous example of circumvallation took place at Alesia in 52 BCE. There, Caesar had his army build a vast ring of siege works around the Gaulish town. He fought off relief forces and attempts to break out of the town, eventually defeating the defenders and breaking the back of Gaulish resistance to Roman rule.

Caesar was also responsible for one of the most ingenious efforts at cutting off supplies. In 50 BCE, his forces besieged Uxellodunum, another Gaulish settlement. This heavily defended town was built around a natural spring that kept the defenders supplied with water. Caesar's engineers tunneled beneath the town and diverted the underground stream feeding the spring. Cut off from water supplies and believing that the gods had turned against them, the Gauls surrendered.

Of course, not all sieges ended so easily for the Romans. Though they cut off supplies and bombarded the defenses, many opponents still held out against them. In those cases, the time eventually came for making an assault.

The Romans had many different methods for assaulting a city. Sometimes, the walls were broken down. Artillery battered at them until a gap was made and troops could attack. Battering rams pounded at the gates, using these weak points as the easiest way in.

Mining was one of the most effective ways of breaking the walls, but one that involved a lot of hard work. The legionaries would dig a tunnel beneath the enemy defenses, holding it up with wooden pit props. Then they would build a fire in the tunnel to destroy those supports. When the tunnel collapsed, it brought down the ground above it and anything built there, including city walls. Roman troops could then charge through the gap. This proved a great success at sieges such as Fidenae in 435 BCE and Piraeus in 86 BCE.

Mining was also useful in circumventing city walls. At Veii in 396 BCE, Camillus had his miners dig a tunnel from his siege lines to the heart of the town. Rather than burn the tunnel down, his troops rushed down it, emerging in the center of the city and taking the defenders by surprise.

The most common way of getting around city walls was to build an assault ramp. This was a solid ramp, usually made from earth, rocks, and timber, which rose from the Roman lines to the top of the enemy walls. One of the biggest challenges when building such a ramp was protecting the builders, as the enemy could see the construction coming and knew that they needed to stop it. But if the ramp could be completed, then it provided a stable route to the top of any defenses. During the siege of Masada in Israel, the Romans built a ramp that let them reach the walls of a supposedly impregnable mountaintop fortress, compelling the Jews inside to commit suicide rather than be conquered.

Andrew Shiva's picture of Masada

Leading an assault was an extremely risky task, as the assault troops had to charge straight at a determined enemy who now had nothing to lose. In recognition of this, the Romans awarded two military decorations to men who led assaults. The corona vallaris, or rampart crown, was awarded to the first man to cross the ramparts, while the corona muralis, or mural crown, was awarded to the first man across the walls. These show the extent to which the Romans valued the courage it took to lead such an assault.

Civilian Roles

In the early days of the Roman army, legionaries served purely as soldiers. They were called up for as long as they were needed to fight a war, then returned to civilian life. However, this changed with the growth of the empire. Defending a big territory meant that the Romans had to have large bodies of troops on standby at all times. To utilize the resources of the state, they also used the soldiers for other duties. They became responsible for both administering the empire and building the physical resources on which it was run.

The regions of the empire were led by men who had both military and civilian responsibilities. These governors led both armies and bureaucracies. They were responsible for raising taxes, keeping the peace, negotiating with local leaders, and keeping their territory safe.

As the governors were military commanders, their staff were drawn from the units under their command. Taken from their regular units for the duration of their role, they became servants to the governor. Some were bodyguards for him, his household, and his staff. Others had less martial roles.

Administrative posts filled by legionaries included the cornicularii (clerks) who provided bureaucratic support for the regional government, the exceptores and notarii, who we would label as secretaries in modern terms, and the adiutores, who were administrative assistants. The exacti and librarii kept records and managed the heaps of documents accumulated by a busy bureaucracy, alongside the commentarienses, who recorded events in the province and maintained those records. Even senior positions such as beneficiarii, frumentarii, and speculatores, the men commanding the machinery of regional government, were drawn from the legions. The men administering the provinces were also the ones defending them.

On a more local level, garrison commanders found themselves lumbered with administrative work. As the most senior imperial figure in his locality, a commander would be caught between the upward flow of requests from locals and the downward trickle of instructions from the governor's office. As the records custodian of census data, he became the centre for local bureaucracy.

In an empire run by its army, soldiers could hardly escape becoming bureaucrats.

There were no police in the Roman world. Instead, the job of maintaining order and asserting the rule of law fell upon imperial administrators and the legionaries serving them. Legions were stationed all over the empire, in part to uphold law and order and to ensure that people felt safe. Garrisons were placed on important roads to deter banditry, letting travelers go by in peace. By making travel safer for merchants and messengers, they helped the imperial economy to grow and the empire to achieve some level of coherence and integration.

Their policing role extended to enforcement as well as deterrence. The remains of records kept on papyri in Egypt show that people often appealed to the commanders of local garrisons to investigate crimes and punish the perpetrators. The crimes they were called in for included assault, theft, and threats. Their monopoly on the use of force meant that the legions were the only ones who could effectively enforce the law.

From the start of their military service, legionaries learned how to build marching camps and siege works. This training made them more experienced in construction. The legions also contained specialists, such as architects and surveyors who oversaw the construction of camps and the engineers who made and maintained the siege machines. As a result, when they weren't at war, the armies of Rome were the perfect workforce for civilian construction projects.

Road building was one of their most important construction tasks. The long, uniform roads for which the empire was known were often built by the legions. This, in turn, helped the armies in their military duties, as they could more easily get from place to place.

Other projects had no military use but were still undertaken by the legions. The creation of a canal at Antioch and the restoration of the aqueduct at Caesarea Maritima were both important civil engineering projects made possible by the skills and labor of the legions.

One of the most famous legionary constructions was Hadrian's Wall, the massive defensive work that marked the northern boundary of Roman Britain, blocking out the barbarians who lived beyond. Three legions stationed in Britain were each assigned a stretch of the wall to build, and this work was further subdivided by giving parts to individual centuries.

A picture of part of Hadrian's Wall

The legions were responsible for manufacturing much of their own equipment rather than relying on civilian contractors. They had their own potteries run and staffed by legionaries, which produced cooking pots and the tiles used in military buildings. These potteries seem to have provided goods for people outside the legions, as tiles marked with the stamp of military units were used in civilian construction.

The production and maintenance of arms and armor was vitally important. Large military camps often had a workshop for this, where legionaries learnt the skills needed to operate a forge.

The army even played a part in obtaining raw materials. They supervised mines and quarries, particularly in dangerous areas such as western Britain. Curtius Rufus, the governor of Upper Germany, had his soldiers labor down in the silver mines, ensuring a steady supply of the precious metal. In the process, he earned himself both a tidy profit and a great deal of prestige.

Thus, even when the legions weren't at war, they were seldom idle.

Politics

"The die is cast." – Caesar upon crossing the Rubicon.

From the late Republic and onward, the armies played an important role in Roman politics. Perhaps the most critical example of this came in 49 BCE, when a civil war that effectively ended the republic.

Caesar had been a prominent leader from the senatorial class, and he had made his name as a military commander, particularly through his hugely successful campaigns against the Gauls. He was popular with his troops, and like many commanders, he had alternated civil and military positions to advance his career.

Caesar's ambitions alarmed many in the Senate, so inevitably, a large group formed to oppose him. They were led by his former ally, Pompey the Great. Despite Caesar's military successes during the Gallic Wars, the political situation in Rome was deteriorating. Caesar had succeeded in securing a confirmation for his posting as governor for a further five years, not least thanks to his considerable military successes, but he was growing ever more estranged from Pompey the Great, who resented the younger man's ascendancy as a general and realized it threatened to eclipse him. When Caesar's daughter Julia, whom he had married to Pompey to cement their alliance before assuming the governorship, died in childbirth, the last link between the two men was severed. And when Crassus was killed campaigning in the East in 53 BCE, the Triumvirate came to an abrupt end.

Caesar wished to return to Rome to establish his political position there, but in 52 BCE. all of Gaul rose up in arms against him under the leadership of Vercingetorix of the Avernii, who was named High King. Vercingetorix turned out to be a canny fighter who avoided open battles against the superior Roman forces, and he even managed to defeat Caesar's men in several skirmishes. Eventually, however, Caesar lay siege to Vercingetorix and his men around Alesia and, despite being attacked front and rear by Vercingetorix's defenders and other Gauls who came to try to lift the siege, succeeded in defeating them both and taking the stronghold. This effectively marked the end of large-scale resistance in Gaul and brought it firmly under Roman control.

By the end of the Gallic wars, the alliance between Caesar and Pompey had devolved from alliance to rivalry, and when his governorship ended in 50 BCE, Pompey was ready to gain an upperhand in Rome. That year, with his term as governor having ended, Caesar received a formal order by the Senate, largely the product of Pompey's machinations, to disband his army and return to Rome, but Caesar was certain that he was going to be held to account for his debts and other irregularities. Assuming that any trial he participated would likely be a witch-hunt specifically designed to permanently tarnish him, he would have none of it.

Clearly the situation in Rome quickly became untenable. Having crossed into Northern Italy, Caesar was encamped close to the northern bank of the Rubicon River. This was a hugely momentous event, as the Rubicon marked the southernmost boundary a general could advance on Rome from the north with his army, and the last people to infringe upon this border had been the military dictators Marius and Sulla, the memory of whose purges was still fresh in the minds of many Romans. If Caesar crossed the river in arms, it would be war. Matters came to a head when the Senate took a vote as to whether Caesar or Pompey should stand down. The optimates wanted Caesar to disarm, the populares wanted Pompey to do the same, and some suggested both generals should dismiss their forces and meet for talks.

Many of the senators accepted this proposal, seeing a chance to be saved from civil war, but Consul Lentulus (the second of the two consuls, along with Marcellus, and also an optimate) refused to let the matter be put to a vote. He shouted Caesar's ally, Mark Antony, down, and instead proposed a motion for martial law to be instituted to counter what he called the threat of Caesar's invasion, a decree which, if passed, would almost certainly mean Pompey's appointment as plenipotentiary dictator.

Since Caesar refused to obey the Senate, Pompey worked to have him accused of treason. Caesar, meanwhile, had taken his own initiative. After much deliberation, he decided that Antony's treatment could mean only that his opponents would never surrender peaceably, and in the spring of 49 BCE. Leaving the majority of his forces in Gaul, Caesar headed south for Italy that January at the head of the 13th Legion, despite repeated remonstrations by the Senate and threats by Pompey. That month, Caesar and his men crossed the Rubicon River into Italy, thus entering Italy as invaders, and it's likely that similar exploits by his uncle Marius and Sulla were playing in his mind. According to Suetonius and Plutarch, as his troops filed by, he famously quoted the Greek playwright Menander, remarking: "The die is cast".

A bust of Pompey

The power of military commanders had created a great dispute within the Roman elite, and now it would settle the issue. Caesar's legions were experienced and intensely loyal to him. Pompey was a gifted commander, but Caesar proved even better. He overran the senatorial forces in Italy and then faced them at Pharsalus in Greece. There, he defeated a larger force led by Pompey. The senatorial faction never again seriously threatened Caesar's dominance, though it took him several years to mop them up and end the war in victory.

Though Caesar was assassinated soon after his victory, he had set a precedent for powerful men to seize control of the empire with their legions after they had been posted far from Rome. As such, the army played an important during periods of instability or uncertainty, and it often decided who would sit on the throne. Caligula and Galba were both assassinated by the elite Praetorian Guard during the 1st century CE. After Galba, his successor Otho committed suicide after being defeated in battle, and by the end of the same year, a third emperor, Vitellius, had been murdered by troops serving Vespasian. Vespasian finally took control as emperor, marking 69 CE as the "Year of the Four Emperors."

The 3rd century CE was a particularly tumultuous period. A string of emperors died in battle or were assassinated by Roman soldiers. To retain power, an emperor needed military might, but the influence of the army could be a destabilizing force. The loyalty of soldiers to their commanders above the rest of Rome led to coups and usurpations.

Marius's mules had made Rome great, but their political influence fostered the instability and divisions that would bring the empire down. Aside from the civil war in 68-69 CE, the empire was mostly stable and internally peaceful from the 1st century BCE to the late 2nd century CE, but then came a period of instability and civil war as men grappled for control of the empire. Legion fought against legion as the empire was ripped apart. Peace was restored late in the 3rd century, but by then outsiders had taken the opportunity to raid deep into the empire, causing permanent changes. The boundaries between civilized Rome and the barbarian world beyond were starting to collapse. Emperor Diocletian divided the empire into two parts, still a single entity but with the east and west led by different men, to try to control an increasingly chaotic situation.

Provinces became smaller and military campaigns more local as commanders fought off barbarian incursions or took part in civil wars. The way the Romans fought was changing, as was the population of the empire, and the army changed to reflect this.

Until the 2nd century CE, political and military leadership were usually combined. The officers commanding the legions were drawn from the senatorial class, the highest rank of Roman society. They alternated periods of military and civilian service. The equestrian class, the next layer down in the Roman elite, had always played a role in military leadership. They generally held more junior posts than the senators. Away from the army, they did not have any political power. They, therefore, had more reason to stick with the military, becoming career officers.

However, in the 2nd century CE, emperors started promoting equestrian officers to command legions and even whole armies. There were many reasons why this happened. As career officers, equestrians had more experience and were likely to work for a longer duration. Their lack of political connections may have made them seem less threatening to the emperor's power, and so safer candidates for promotion. They may have been more willing to take on these roles, as they had no political career in Rome to worry about.

A range of new officers appeared, with titles such as praepositi, primicerius, and centenarii. Records for this period are not as good as they were in earlier periods, so it's not clear exactly what all these different officers did, but the overall picture is of a command structure that was increasingly fractured and varied.

The rise of the equestrians was not the boon that some emperors might have expected. Using the support of the men they led, equestrians sought to gain political power. A group of officers stationed in the Danubian provinces rose up in the late 3rd century CE, overthrowing and enthroning a series of emperors.

The leadership of the army was increasingly divided within itself and separated from the leadership of the state. At the same time, the makeup of the ordinary troops serving in the army also changed. By the 4th century CE, an increasingly large part of the Roman armed forces was made up of outsiders, men the Romans themselves labeled as barbarians. Some were recruits drawn from beyond the boundaries of the empire, while others came from tribes who had been allowed to migrate into Roman territory, where they were granted land in return for military service. There were even prisoners of war, turned into imperial soldiers and sent to defend territory far from where they were captured.

The use of outsiders was not new; after all, the auxiliaries had always provided cavalry and light troops drawn from outside the pool of Roman citizens. But the scale of recruitment was different, and barbarians increasingly came to dominate the army. This was exacerbated by the use of units called foederati, in which barbarian tribal leaders led their own men, instead of having them serve under Roman officers.

The cultural, ethnic, and social mix of the army was more diverse than ever. It was no longer a force of citizens with a deep and enduring attachment to Rome. Instead, it was a hotchpotch of men who might care little about the fate of the empire. They were not rewarded for its successes, and so had little reason to worry if it collapsed.

The equipment used by Roman soldiers also became more diverse in the final centuries of the empire. One example was the changing place of archery in the Roman armed forces. By the 4th century, archery had become a suitable skill for an aristocratic officer or even an emperor. New types of bows and saddles were adopted from the Huns, along with the tactics they used. Horse archers became an important part of some Roman armies, even serving as the core of the battle line, a place previously reserved for traditionally equipped legionaries.

Cavalry were increasingly prominent within Roman armies. Whether they were more numerous or tactically important is unclear, but they certainly rose in prestige. Europe's feudal elite of heavily armored knights descended from these prominent cavalry units.

Even the equipment of the core legionaries changed. Segmented armor almost entirely vanished. The gladius was replaced by the long-bladed sword called a spatha, the rectangular shield by a round one. Most soldiers no longer carried javelins. The Roman troops of the late empire looked more and more like the local warbands who would replace them in the Dark Ages.

One of the most important changes among the ordinary soldiers was their division into two types of units - comitatensis and limitanei. The comitatensis were field troops, sent out on campaign against Rome's enemies. Limitanei were garrison forces, most often found in border regions. Theirs was a stationary, defensive role, sitting in the same post for years on end, unlike the dynamic activity of the comitatensis and the earlier legions. As the most politically and military powerful force in an area, they became the local elite, a pattern of social leadership by military forces that was followed by medieval warbands.

Changes in the empire had forced the Roman army to change. But this undermined the discipline and unity that had made the legions so strong. Large campaigns gave way to local raiding as the powerful central drive of the empire was lost and Rome went into decline.

The Roman army was the most disciplined and powerful in the ancient world. Centrally organized and tightly controlled, it was like no other force it ran up against, and its strength carved out an empire of unprecedented scale and wealth. At the same time, the army was deeply tied to the society it defended. Soldiers provided the engineers and administrators who kept Rome's vast territories working.

However, much as the Romans lived by the sword, they also died by the sword, and the policies they implemented to make their army the world's elite fighting force also sowed some of the seeds of their own empire's destruction. The makeup of the armies reflected changes in society, but it also triggered them, leading to the rise and fall of emperors.

In the whole of European history, no army has been as influential or as iconic as that of Rome. The lessons of its leaders echo down to the modern day. They came, they saw, they conquered, and in the process they changed the world.

Online Resources

Other books about ancient history by Charles River Editors

Other books about ancient Rome by Charles River Editors

Other books about the Roman Army on Amazon

Further Reading

Ancient Texts

Anonymous, *Lindian Chronicle*. C. Higbie. 2003. *The Lindian Chronicle and the Greek Creation of their Past.* London: Oxford University Press.

Anonymous, *Oxyrhynchus Hellenica*. B.P. Grenfell, A.S. Hunt. 1898. *Oxyrhynchus Papyri.* n. 26. London: Egypt Exploration Fund.

Diodorus Siculus, *Library of History*. C.H. Oldfather. 1935. *Library of History.* Cambridge, MA: Harvard University Press. The text, supplemented from older translations with those sections of the work not available in the public domain, is available online at: http://penelope.uchicago.edu/Thayer/E/Roman/Texts/Diodorus_Siculus/home.html

Herodotus, *Histories.* A.D. Godley. 1920. *Herodotus, with an English translation by A. D. Godley.* Cambridge, MA: Harvard University Press.

Titus Livius, *The History of Rome.* B.J. Butterfield. 1996. Available online at:

http://mcadams.posc.mu.edu/txt/ah/Livy/

Pindar, *Paeans*. I. Rutherford 2001. *A Reading of the Fragments with a Survey of the Genre*. Oxford: Clarendon Press.

Polybius, *Histories*. E.S. Shuckburgh, 1889. *The Histories of Polybius, 2 Vols*. London: Macmillan.

Strabo, *Geography*. H.C. Hamilton, W. Falconer. 1903. *The Geography of Strabo. Literally translated, with notes, in three volumes*. London: George Bell & Sons.

Thucydides *Histories*. B. Jowett. 1881. *Thucydides translated into English; with introduction, marginal analysis, notes, and indices*. Oxford: Clarendon Press.

Xenophon, *Hellenica*. C.L. Brownson. 1918-1921. *Xenophon. Xenophon in Seven Volumes, 1 and 2*. Cambridge, MA: Harvard University Press; London: William Heinemann, Ltd.

Modern Sources

d'Agostino, B. 2006. "Funerary customs and society on Rhodes in the Geometric Period: some observations," in Herring, E. and Lemos, I (eds). *Across Frontiers: Etruscans, Greeks, Phoenicians and Cypriots. Studies in Honour of D. Ridgway and F.R. Serra Ridgway* 57-69. London: Accordia Research Institute, University of London.

Bozeman, A.B. 1994. *Politics and Culture in International History: From the Ancient Near East to the Opening of the Modern Age*. New Jersey: Transaction Publishers.

Bosworth, A.B. 2012. "Memnon (2)," in *The Oxford Classical Dictionary (4th edition)*. London: Oxford University Press.

Brodersen, K. 2007. "Aegean Greece," in Kinzl, K., *A Companion to the Classical Greek World*. Malden, MA: Blackwell Publishing.

Cadoux, T.J., Seager, R.J. 2012. "Cassius Longinus (1) Gaius," in Hornblower, S., Spawforth, N., Eidinow, E. *The Oxford Classical Dictionary (4th edition)*. London: Oxford University Press.

Cawkwell, G.L. 2012a. "Chabrias," in *The Oxford Classical Dictionary (4th edition)*. London: Oxford University Press.

Cawkwell, G.L. 2012b. "Chares," in *The Oxford Classical Dictionary (4th edition)*. London: Oxford University Press.

Derow, P. 2003. "The Arrival of the Romans: from the Illyrian War to the Fall of Macedon," in Erskine, A. *A Companion to the Hellenistic World*. London: Blackwell.

Duncan-Jones, R. 2002. *Structure and Scale in the Roman Economy*. Cambridge: Cambridge University Press.

Griffiths, A. 2012. "Telchines," in Hornblower, S., Spawforth, N., Eidinow, E. *The Oxford Classical Dictionary (4th edition)*. London: Oxford University Press.

Higbie, C. 2003. *The Lindian Chronicle and the Greek Creation of their Past*. London: Oxford University Press.

Howatson, M.C. 2011. *The Oxford Companion to Classical Literature (3rd edition)*. London: Oxford University Press.

Lazenby, J.F. 2012a. "Persian Wars," in Hornblower, S., Spawforth, N., Eidinow, E. *The Oxford Classical Dictionary (4th edition)*. London: Oxford University Press.

Lazenby, J.F. 2012b. "Peloponnesian Wars," in Holmes, R., Singleton, C., Jones, S. *The Oxford Companion to Military History*. London: Oxford University Press.

Martin, T. 2010. "Antigonus Monophthalmus," in Gagarin, M., Fantham, E. *Oxford Encyclopedia of Ancient Greece and Rome*. London, New York: Oxford University Press.

Mee, C.B., Rice, E. 1998. "Rhodes," in Hornblower, S. Spawforth, N. *The Oxford Companion to Classical Civilization (1st edition)*. London: Oxford University Press.

Meiggs, R., Hornblower, S. 1998. "Delian League," in Hornblower, S. Spawforth, N. *The Oxford Companion to Classical Civilization (1st edition)*. London: Oxford University Press.

Smith, W. (ed.). 1857. "Doric Hexapolis," in *Dictionary of Greek and Roman Geography*. London: John Murray.

Smith, W. (ed.). 1849. "Rhode," in *Dictionary of Greek and Roman Biography and Biology*. Boston: Little Brown and Company.

Stuard, A.F. 2012. "Chares (4)," in Hornblower, S., Spawforth, N., Eidinow, E. *The Oxford Classical Dictionary (4th edition)*. London: Oxford University Press.

Tomlinson, R, Spawforth, A. 2012 "Hippodamus of Miletus," in Hornblower, S., Spawforth, N., Eidinow, E. *The Oxford Classical Dictionary (4th edition)*. London: Oxford University Press.

Trichas, A. 2004. "Biogeography of the Aegean," in Efthimiopoulos, I., Modinos, M. (supervisors). *The nature of geography*. Athens: Interdisciplinary Institute for Environmental Research, pp. 379.

Walbank, F.W. 1940. *Philip V of Macedon*. Cambridge: Cambridge University Press.

Westlake, H.D. 1983. "Conon and Rhodes: the Troubled Aftermath of Synoecism." *Greek, Roman and Byzantine Studies*, 24:4 (1983: Winter): 333 334.

Wheatley, P. 2010. "Diadochi and Successor Kingdoms," in Gagarin, M., Fantham, E. *Oxford Encyclopedia of Ancient Greece and Rome*. London, New York: Oxford University Press.

Free Books by Charles River Editors

We have brand new titles available for free most days of the week. To see which of our titles are currently free, click on this link.

Discounted Books by Charles River Editors

We have titles at a discount price of just 99 cents everyday. To see which of our titles are currently 99 cents, click on this link.

Made in the USA
Middletown, DE
22 December 2021